Grieving with

hope

LEANING ON JESUS

Tim Wesemann

cta
Christ to All

The vision of CTA is
to see Christians highly effective
in their ministries so that Christ's Kingdom
is strengthened and expanded.

Grieving with hope

LEANING ON JESUS

Tim Wesemann

Copyright © 2022 CTA, Inc.
1653 Larkin Williams Rd.
Fenton, MO 63026
ctainc.com

Unless otherwise indicated, Scripture quotations are from the ESV® Bible
(The Holy Bible, English Standard Version®), copyright © 2001 by Crossway,
a publishing ministry of Good News Publishers. Used by permission.
All rights reserved.

ISBN: 978-1-947699-53-3
PRINTED IN USA

The LORD is near to the brokenhearted and saves the crushed in spirit.

Psalm 34 : 18

Heartbroken.

Crushed in spirit.

Those feelings often accompany grief. Maybe they have taken up residence in your life. As familiar as those feelings might be at this time, I pray something else also resides within you besides your pain caused by grief.

Hope

Christian hope isn't a wishful kind of hope. It's the sure-and-certain hope that comes from the One who embodies the gift. Jesus Christ not only provides hope, he *is* hope. He is your hope, even in your grief.

You may experience times when your hurt doesn't want to hear about hope. Maybe you won't allow yourself that hope, wrongly thinking it will drown out the grieving you want and need to experience.

You will likely also experience times when the relentless ache seems greater than the hope. At times, it will appear that God himself and any hope you ever once held on to have walked out of your life. Truth tells another story in the book of Romans.

For I am sure that neither death nor life, nor angels nor rulers, nor things present nor things to come, nor powers, nor height nor depth, nor anything else in all creation, will be able to separate us from the love of God in Christ Jesus our Lord.

Romans 8 : 38–39

You can grasp that good news by faith, which the Book of Hebrews defines as "the assurance of things hoped for, the conviction of things not seen" (Hebrews 11:1). You can be sure of God's hope, even during times it seems to hide in a fog of grief.

So what is this hope—this sure-and-certain hope—your Savior has for you?

Hope for Here and Now

- God will never leave you or forsake you (Deuteronomy 31:6).
- Jesus gives peace beyond your comprehension, and not a temporary peace like the world offers, but permanent, eternal peace (John 14:27).
- You can approach God in prayer freely and confidently through Christ and expect his help (Ephesians 3:12).
- You can do all things *through Christ* who strengthens you (Philippians 4:13).

With those promises in mind, Paul reminds you that as a child of God you don't have to grieve like those who have no hope (1 Thessalonians 4:13). Certainly you will grieve, but you do so with the confidence that the "LORD is near to the brokenhearted and saves the crushed in spirit" (Psalm 34:18).

Brokenhearted . . . but not without hope.
Crushed in spirit . . . but not without hope.

If you're finding it difficult to hold on to hope, know that Jesus and the unending hope he gives are holding on to you. Lean into it. Lean on Jesus. Allow his love to calm your restlessness as he whispers words of love, strength, and hope into your life.

We are afflicted in every way, but not crushed; perplexed, but not driven to despair; persecuted, but not forsaken; struck down, but not destroyed.

2 Corinthians 4 : 8—9

You may experience times when your hurt doesn't want to hear about hope.

Concluding Prayer

Jesus, I ache.

Emotionally. Physically. Spiritually.

I hear you are close to the brokenhearted.

I need you close to me.

Hold me. Help me. Bring me hope.

As I lean on you, quiet me in your love,

whispering your promises of hope into my life.

Yes, Jesus, I ache.

My heart aches for you.

My heart aches for your hope and help.

I trust you . . . even in my grief.

Amen.

Chapter Two

Talking Honestly with Your Savior-Friend

> May the God of hope fill you with all joy and peace in believing, so that by the power of the Holy Spirit you may abound in hope.
>
> Romans 15:13

Jesus Knows—and Cares!

Jesus hears your every expression of grief—spoken and unspoken. He's familiar with the unspoken expressions contained in your wordless sighs, the sound of your falling tears, and your soul's cry of "Why?"

As you lean on him, he wants you to speak honestly and openly with him. He not only wants you to experience the healing that comes from sharing your hurts with him; he also wants to comfort you in the truth that he does always listen. In love, he offers help and hope.

As you talk honestly with the Lord, you'll find you have a lot in common with those who wrote the Old Testament psalms. Their honest and straightforward words flow from hearts surrounded by brokenness yet saturated with the presence of a loving God.

Psalm 13 offers a great example. As David expresses his anger, fear, and abandonment, he doesn't mince words. He feels God has walked away from him and can't be found. He writes of agonizing struggles within his mind and body.

In his weakened state, feeling defeated and deflated, David is on the verge of giving up. Maybe you can relate.

Telling the Whole Truth

But after having told the truth about his pain, David pauses. Leaning on the Lord, he has spoken honestly and boldly. But he knows in his heart there's more to the story. He grieves over his situation, all the while knowing hope comes from the Lord, his God. Therefore, the psalm ends with these words of truth, spoken by David amidst his grief:

But I have trusted in your steadfast love;
my heart shall rejoice in your salvation.
I will sing to the LORD,
because he has dealt bountifully with me.

Psalm 13:5–6

The Lord knows you are hurt. Approach him with boldness. As you talk openly and honestly with him, realize it's okay to ask "Why?" It's natural that you have questions—questions you'd like answered!

The reality is that suffering, pain, and even death are results of sin in our world. Sometimes that's the only answer we will receive to our many questions. Between the perfection of the Garden of Eden and the perfection of heaven lies a chasm filled with sin. Our world is broken.

But it's also a world filled with the hope, help, and comfort of Jesus Christ, who leads us every moment. How thankful we can be that we can lean on and learn from our Savior of hope.

Jesus Invites Your Trust

While Jesus invites your questions and wants you to cast your cares on him, he also wants to invite your trust. Questioning the Lord can lead you to search his Word to discern his ways and in doing that, grow closer to him. Or it can drive you farther from his presence.

Knowing that, go ahead and question—but keep on trusting God to provide answers. Go ahead and question—but keep on holding firmly to his promises. Go ahead and question—but keep on leaning on his presence.

Jesus is listening, even when the words aren't there. Lean on Jesus. Share your pain honestly, trusting him in it because . . .

We know that for those who love God all things work together for good, for those who are called according to his purpose.

Romans 8:28

Jesus hears your every expression of grief— spoken and unspoken.

Concluding Prayer

Jesus, I find it difficult to pray at times.

I don't have the words.

I don't know what to pray for.

Sometimes my prayers sound selfish.

I'm going to trust that even when I don't know what to pray, the Holy Spirit is taking my wordless sighs and unspoken thoughts and shaping them into a perfect prayer. He will present them to the Father in your name.

Your promises continue to hold me together.

And I know your grace is sufficient for me. Amen.

Chapter Three

Listening with Hope

Trust in the LORD with all your heart, and do not lean on your own understanding. In all your ways acknowledge him, and he will make straight your paths.

Proverbs 3:5–6

When It's Hard to Listen

Many times, those who grieve find it easier to pray than to listen for God's answers. Maybe you are finding it easier to cry out, even in anger and accusations, than to wait for his response. At some point in the grieving process, you may decide the search for answers is futile as you turn instead to find someone to blame. At that point, perhaps God himself will seem to be the easiest, most appropriate target.

No matter what, you can be certain that Jesus understands. Allow him to respond to your pleas. Truly listen to him. Lean on him during your grief.

Are you asking *how* God will respond? Do you wonder *how* you will hear? Just as you communicate with him in a variety of ways, he responds in a variety of ways as well.

Never Alone

First, Jesus doesn't want you to go through this season of grief on your own. The Lord clearly communicates with you through his Word. He will use that Word to assure you of his sustaining promises, love, and hope.

As you read Scripture verses from this book and other Christ-centered materials, you'll realize his unlimited and unconditional love for you—personally and powerfully for you.

Your Lord will also speak his peace to you through faith-filled people who point you to Jesus, your Savior, and who share his love for you through their own compassionate acts of love.

Be Still and Know . . .

s difficult as it may be at this moment, be still. Even though your eart and mind are restless in your grief, be still and listen. Lean n Jesus. Let him take you into his arms and calm you, as you sten to his words of hope, help, and life!

Lean on Jesus and listen.

Come to me, all who labor and are heavy laden, and I will give you rest. Take my yoke upon you, and learn from me, for I am gentle and lowly in heart, and you will find rest for your souls.

Matthew 11 : 28–29

Lean on Jesus and listen.

My grace is sufficient for you, for my power is made perfect in weakness.

2 Corinthians 12 : 9

ean on Jesus and listen.

, the LORD your God, hold your right hand;
t is I who say to you, "Fear not, I am the
ne who helps you."

Isaiah 41:13

isten. Your Savior loves you.

Even though your heart and mind are restless in your grief, be still and listen.

Concluding Prayer

Talk to me, Lord.

I'm trying to hear you,

trying to be aware of your presence.

It's hard to concentrate,

but I know you're near.

I still don't understand it all.

Maybe I never will this side of heaven.

Help me to hear you speak to me.

Help me recall Bible passages

or hymn verses or songs of hope

I've heard in the past.

I'm listening. I know you're speaking.

Comfort me with your words of love. Amen.

Chapter Four

So Many Emotions!

And the peace of God, which surpasses all understanding, will guard your hearts and your minds in Christ Jesus.

Philippians 4:7

You may never experience a wider range of emotions than while grieving the death of someone you love. At times your tears may flow freely and frequently. Other times you may experience the sadness just as deeply but without tears. You may choose to cry with family and friends. Or you may grieve in solitude instead. Since we're all created differently, grief manifests itself in different ways for each individual.

Tears, Sadness, and . . . ?

This highly charged, emotional time comes packed with tears and deep sadness. But as you grieve, you may also be blessed to experience joy and laughter as you remember your loved one. Telling stories and remembering fun experiences can take you from tears to smiles and even laughter in a matter of seconds. You may be deeply touched as people share how the one you loved made a powerful impact on their lives in ways you never knew before.

Expect times of overwhelming peace as well as feelings of hurt and anger. And don't be surprised if at times you feel nothing—as though every emotion has dried up and you're living on autopilot.

Emotions and Their Triggers

You've probably noticed that your emotions erupt at the oddest of times and places. Many times, memories pop up unexpectedly, perhaps triggered by something as simple as seeing a favorite breakfast cereal in your grocery store or driving past a particular highway exit or being seated at the same restaurant table where you and your loved one once shared a meal.

Our Lord created and gifted all of us with emotions. Suppressing them or allowing them to overpower you will harm you physically, mentally, and spiritually. Don't stifle those feelings. Embrace the joyful memories. Keep them alive and allow God to use them in your healing.

While emotions in and of themselves aren't sinful, it's possible to allow them to lead you across the line drawn between a healthy outlook and a sinful attitude or action. For instance, anger isn't a sin; it's an emotion. But the way you respond to anger can help or harm you and those around you.

Depression often associates itself with grief. In most cases after the death of a loved one, it's short term and situational. Yet sometimes an extended, deep depression can develop.

So if you experience a depression that drags on, don't be ashamed to seek professional help.

A Miracle of Joy

Surprisingly, our Lord often works a miraculous peace and sometimes even an inner joy in the midst of our tears. That peace comes from and through Jesus Christ. It comes from the certain knowledge of his unshakable, unchanging love. It comes from the hope that one day our Savior will wipe away every tear from our eyes:

Death shall be no more, neither shall there be mourning, nor crying, nor pain anymore, for the former things [will have] passed away.

Revelation 21:4

Jesus wants his love for you to be your foundation as he walks with you through this emotion-filled season of grief.

Expect times of overwhelming peace as well as feelings of hurt and anger.

Concluding Prayer

"Jesus wept" (John 11:35).

I've known that verse for years—it's

the shortest in the Bible, I'm told.

It has special meaning to me now.

Tears flow easily these days . . .

and at the oddest of times!

Sometimes I feel guilty laughing

and enjoying life; yet I know it's okay.

Sometimes people seem uncomfortable around

me, wondering what to say or what to do.

I feel uncomfortable around you sometimes, Lord.

Your love is unconditional and constant.

I have nothing to fear.

Make me comfortable

as I lean on you and rely on you.

Through tears and all, you know I love you, Jesus.

Thank you for your love.

You cried. I cry.

That makes me very comfortable. Amen.

Chapter Five

The Gift of Forgiveness

Likewise the Spirit helps us in our weakness. For we do not know what to pray for as we ought, but the Spirit himself intercedes for us with groanings too deep for words. And he who searches hearts knows what is the mind of the Spirit, because the Spirit intercedes for the saints according to the will of God. And we know that for those who love God all things work together for good, for those who are called according to his purpose.

Romans 8 : 26–28

Forgiveness and grief. While these two might seem an unlikely pair, even in times of grief it's comforting to know God freely gives his gift of forgiveness.

While you grieve, you might feel overwhelmed with guilt. You might find yourself dredging up past sins, even the forgiven ones. You might experience the emotions God gave you for your good and use them in a sinful way. For all these reasons, it's important—even as we grieve—to remember God's gift of forgiveness and the comfort he brings through that freeing gift.

The "If Onlys"

One of your first responses to your loved one's death may have been guilt. Death catches us off guard, and we immediately have thoughts like these:

- "If only I had . . ."
- "I should have . . . "
- "What if . . .?"
- "Could I have done something . . .?"
- "Am I to blame for . . .?"
- "I hate that I responded the way I did the last time we . . ."
- "I'll never forget that bad memory when . . ."

In reality most of your guilt isn't *sin*-based. It's not something for which you need God's pardon. It's *grief*-based guilt that wishes you had done more or done some things differently.

n times like that, you have a choice.
ou can allow yourself to wallow in guilt
nstead of grieving in hope. You can
hoose to let guilt drag you down, or you
an allow Jesus to sustain you and carry
ou through this difficult time.

You can't go back and change anything you did or left undone. But you can go to the cross of Jesus and let him change your life, your heart. You can focus on everything he did on the cross, leaving nothing undone.

In your imagination, walk to the cross. Yes, it's a place of death. But it's truly also the place of new life. See Jesus' empty Easter tomb in the background? Confess your real sins there. Hear his words of undeserved love as he forgives all your sins. His words aren't hollow; his forgiveness is real and total. Repentant, lean on Jesus for full forgiveness.

Receive and Remember

As you receive his forgiveness, remember that when God forgives your sins, he remembers them no more (Isaiah 43:25; Psalm 103:12). It's true. God's forgiving amnesia is another of his gifts to you as you grieve with hope.

So don't let your past sins haunt you! Since God has completely forgiven you through Jesus' death and resurrection, you can also forgive yourself. And you can forgive others, too, just as you have been forgiven.

Don't live in guilt. Live in God's grace. Don't walk with regret. Walk with your resurrected Redeemer. Don't lean on your own understanding. Lean on Jesus, who understands your need for his salvation.

ou are free. Free from guilt. Free to
rieve—with hope and peace from Jesus.

Don't live in guilt. Live in God's grace.

Concluding Prayer

Some days, Savior, guilt brings me down.

I keep thinking there is something . . .

I don't know.

Something I could have said.

Something I could have done.

Something.

Sometimes people get on my nerves.

I'm short with them, impatient.

I know they want to help.

If I've sinned against you or others,

know that I am truly sorry.

Humbled, I ask for and accept your forgiveness.

Help me forgive myself and others

just as you have forgiven me.

I can't imagine how I'd make it from

moment to moment without your grace.

Forgiven and loved, I thank you, my Savior. Amen

Chapter Six

Learning from Others

The LORD is my shepherd; I shall not want. He makes me lie down in green pastures. He leads me beside still waters. He restores my soul. He leads me in paths of righteousness for his name's sake. Even though I walk through the valley of the shadow of death, I will fear no evil, for you are with me; your rod and your staff, they comfort me. You prepare a table before me in the presence of my enemies; you anoint my head with oil; my cup overflows. Surely goodness and mercy shall follow me all the days of my life, and I shall dwell in the house of the LORD forever.

Psalm 23

How have you learned about grief? Through what lenses and unique experiences have you seen it? How has that shaped you?

Our unique backgrounds make it impossible for one person to say to another in honesty, "I understand" or "I know just how you feel." Others don't know how we feel. (Though some people may still say they do.) On the other hand, it can help to remember that God has given you friends, some of whom have been through their own times of grief. God may use them as a great blessing and help as they walk beside you through this season of your life.

The God of All Comfort

Consider the comforting and wise insight the apostle Paul wrote to the Corinthians.

Blessed be the God and Father of our Lord Jesus Christ, the Father of mercies and God of all comfort, who comforts us in all our affliction, so that we may be able to comfort those who are in any affliction, with the comfort with which we ourselves are comforted by God.

2 Corinthians 1: 3—4

You're one of those going through hard times right now. Whom has God brought alongside you to comfort and help you? Be assured that God will use others if you'll allow him to do that. And if you are available, he will also use you to bless others. Maybe instead of using others, or in addition to using them, God will use articles, books, or stories to teach you about this time in your life.

The brokenhearted people the Scriptures tell us about offer their counsel and comfort. Job and his wife, who suffered their own season of deep grief, serve as an example. They enjoyed ten children, great wealth, and a blessed life. But all of that disappeared in a single day. Their world crumbled, but what happened to their faith?

After losing everything, Job held firmly to his belief in God's goodness as he proclaimed through his tears, "The LORD gave, and the LORD has taken away; blessed be the name of the LORD" (Job 1:21). Job praised God's name even while he sank into the deepest grief! Job's heart wasn't callous; it ached, just as ours would, as he grieved the loss of his family and all he'd had. Yet his faith remained intact.

Lean into Jesus

Jesus, too, faced grief in a spiritually and emotionally healthy way. He wept over the spiritual death of Jerusalem (Luke 19:41). He cried at the tomb of his friend Lazarus (John 11:1–45). He agonized as he faced his own impending death (Luke 22:39–44).

And still, in his grief, Jesus focused on his heavenly Father, on the Father's love for him, and on his mission to rescue you from sin and, yes, from death itself. He grieved while keeping his focus on his cross, empty tomb, and return to heaven to prepare a place for his people.

Learn from others as you grieve.

Learn from Jesus.

Lean on Jesus.

[He] is near to the brokenhearted and saves the crushed in spirit.

Psalm 34:18

Whom has God brought alongside you to comfort and help you?

Concluding Prayer

Lord, I've been going on and on about myself—
my needs, my wants, my pain.
I want to stop and thank you.
Thank you, dear Jesus, for

- my family and friends;
- my church family;
- the comfort you've given me;
- forgiving me;
- putting up with me;
- lessons I've learned and all that you want to teach me;
- your gift of heaven; and
- reminding me that this is not the end because you are a God—the God—who has defeated death.

Thank you, Jesus . . . for all the blessings you've wrapped in hope and left on the doorstep of my heart. May I never take them for granted. Amen.

Chapter Seven

A Holy Silence

Do not be anxious about anything, but in everything by prayer and supplication with thanksgiving let your requests be made known to God. And the peace of God, which surpasses all understanding, will guard your hearts and your minds in Christ Jesus.

Philippians 4:6–7

Silence can be deafening.

Silence can also be holy.

When you're looking for answers and help, and it appears as if God's only reply is silence, then perhaps quiet doesn't equal tranquility. Or does it?

As you lean in faith on Jesus in the quietness of the moment, he will give you peace in the holy silence.

Be Still and Know . . .

Your Lord is close to the brokenhearted. His love for you makes it impossible for him to walk away and leave you isolated, alone. Yet in his love for you, at times his response is silence. He can use those times to teach you about patience and trust. You may need the opportunity those times offer to reflect on God's faithfulness in the past and his promise that even in the stillness, he is close. "I will never leave you nor forsake you" (Hebrews 13:5). In love, he will comfort you through his silent presence.

Jeremiah carries the nickname "the weeping prophet" because of the lifelong grief he experienced. His journal of mourning is known as *The Lamentations of Jeremiah*, or simply *Lamentations*. Throughout this book of the Bible, Jeremiah grieves the loss of Jerusalem, his home. He cries over its brokenness, its sinfulness, and its destruction. He can't grasp why God would have allowed this to happen.

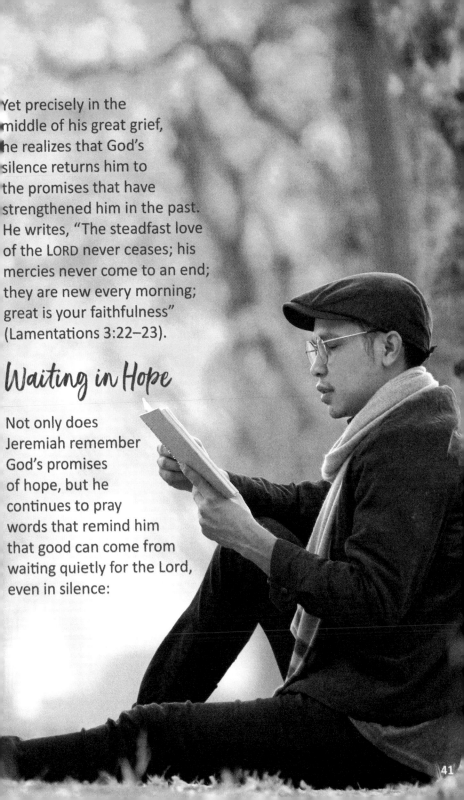

Yet precisely in the middle of his great grief, he realizes that God's silence returns him to the promises that have strengthened him in the past. He writes, "The steadfast love of the LORD never ceases; his mercies never come to an end; they are new every morning; great is your faithfulness" (Lamentations 3:22–23).

Waiting in Hope

Not only does Jeremiah remember God's promises of hope, but he continues to pray words that remind him that good can come from waiting quietly for the Lord, even in silence:

The LORD is good to those who wait for him,
    to the soul who seeks him.
It is good that one should wait quietly
    for the salvation of the LORD.
It is good for a man that he bear
    the yoke in his youth.
Let him sit alone in silence
    when it is laid on him;
let him put his mouth in the dust—
    there may yet be hope;
let him give his cheek to the one who strikes,
    and let him be filled with insults.
For the Lord will not
    cast off forever.

Lamentations 3 : 25—31

Silence can serve as a blessing. The man named Job experienced a holy silence of a different kind. Grieving the loss of his family, Job sat in silence. Three of his friends came to visit, hoping to comfort him. When they saw him, they began to cry, realizing his intense grief. They responded with holy silence. Scripture describes that visit: "They sat with him on the ground seven days and seven nights, and no one spoke a word to him, for they saw that his suffering was very great" (Job 2:13).

Yes, silence can be deafening. But silence can also be holy.

May yours be holy and help you live wholly.

Even in the stillness, God is close.

Concluding Prayer

Sometimes it's too silent.

It makes me feel alone, and often sad.

But I can also say I need your holy silence.

The kind where you just sit with me quietly, Lord.

The kind where I know you are near.

The kind where I know you are working for my

good, even when I don't have a clue.

I want to be still and simply know

that you are God.

You are my God, my Savior, my Friend.

Even when you are silent,

I will trust you.

Quiet me with your love.

Sit with me.

Quiet me.

You are God. Shhh.

You are my God. Shhh.

I find my rest in you.

Shhh.

Chapter Eight

Traveling through the Changes

Truly, truly, I say to you, whoever hears my word and believes him who sent me has eternal life. He does not come into judgment, but has passed from death to life.

John 5:24

The death of a loved one brings about many changes—some extreme, some not. But combined, the changes and the decisions they bring into life can fly at you from every direction. Suddenly your path through life takes a sharp turn, and you find yourself trying to maneuver the hairpin curves of a steep mountain. The path grows steeper and narrower, and there's no place or time to catch your breath.

Facing challenges like that, you can find help by looking into life's rearview mirror. Consider past heartaches and hardships. Remember that every time, the Lord led you *through* life's changes. In the Old Testament, the Lord reminded his people, "When you pass *through* the waters, I will be with you; and *through* the rivers, they shall not overwhelm you; when you walk through fire you shall not be burned, and the flame shall not consume you" (Isaiah 43:2, emphasis added).

Coming Through

The Lord not only promises his presence in times of pain and grief, he also vows to bring his people *through* the difficulties they're facing. That means he can also bring you through this time of change. And while you're facing countless changes, he reminds you that *he* does not change (Malachi 3:6). You can count on his changeless faithfulness no matter what.

As you and I face the end of our life's journey, our Good Shepherd promises, "Even though I walk *through* the valley of the shadow of death, I will fear no evil, for you are with me" (Psalm 23:4, emphasis added).

We will walk *through* the shadow of death because of what Jesus did for us on his cross and in his open tomb.

Change and Final Victory

The apostle Paul saw the Lord bring him through countless difficult circumstances and significant life changes. Having Christ's promise as his foundation, Paul knew he could trust the Lord to bring him through the final leg of his journey.

He poignantly wrote, "I have fought the good fight, I have finished the race, I have kept the faith. Henceforth there is laid up for me the crown of righteousness, which the Lord, the righteous judge, will award to me on that day, and not only to me but also to all who have loved his appearing" (2 Timothy 4:7–8).

Paul knew his Savior had brought him *through* a lifetime of adventures and changes—some unexpected, some expected. And now Jesus would take him through death and on into a perfect eternity in heaven—God's ultimate gift of grace. There Paul would receive the crown of righteousness, all because Jesus had journeyed *through* life, *through* death, and *through* a tomb. Your changeless God will see you through this, too.

A perfect eternity in heaven—
God's ultimate gift of grace

Your changeless God will see you through this, too.

Concluding Prayer

Lord, I had no idea I'd have to make
so many decisions.
Give me wisdom and a clear mind.
Quiet my anxious thoughts with your love so I can
trust you even while decisions and changes run
rampant in my life.
Sometimes I feel they are going to overtake me,
making me a prisoner in my own life
I'm so thankful that the battle is yours
and that your faithfulness and promises have never
changed, nor will they ever change.
Change me so that I rest in your presence,
even when I'm surrounded by change.
I'm leaning on you.
Your wisdom.
Your help.
Your peace.
I need you . . . and here you are.
I love you.

Chapter Nine

Moving Forward by God's Grace

Have you not known? Have you not heard?
The LORD is the everlasting God,
the Creator of the ends of the earth.
He does not faint or grow weary;
his understanding is unsearchable.
He gives power to the faint,
and to him who has no might he increases strength.
Even youths shall faint and be weary,
and young men shall fall exhausted;
but they who wait for the LORD shall
renew their strength;
they shall mount up with wings like eagles;
they shall run and not be weary;
they shall walk and not faint.

Isaiah 40:28–31

As your days, so shall your strength be.
Deuteronomy 33 : 25

What a great promise! Receive that gift from heaven and hide it in your heart. Wake up each day with those words on your lips. Let them reverberate in your thoughts throughout the day, and lie down each night thanking God for providing the strength you needed that day and for each day of your life.

The Lord—My Strength

The Lord will not only *provide* enough strength to carry you through the day, the Lord himself *is* your strength. He makes it possible for you to move forward day after day. Elijah's life provides a good example of this truth.

1 Kings 19 chronicles a segment of Elijah's life in which God's prophet finds himself completely drained of energy. He is running on the fumes of hope. Discouraged, dejected, and depressed, he plops down under a tree and falls asleep. But the Lord isn't going to leave his dearly loved servant in that state. He sends an angel to awaken Elijah, providing him bread and water. After eating, Elijah falls asleep again. The angel comes back with more sustenance, saying, "Arise and eat, for the journey is too great for you" (1 Kings 19:7).

The Lord knows the journey is too much for Elijah to handle alone. And so God rescues, provides for, and strengthens his servant. Scripture tells us Elijah "arose and ate and drank, and went in the strength of that food forty days and forty nights to Horeb, the mount of God" (1 Kings 19:8).

Too Much for Me

It's no different for you. Life's journey is too much for you, too—on your own.

But you're not on your own. You're not alone. God strengthens you through his Word. He sends you encouragement through his people who hurt for you and with you. His presence and his blessing give you peace (Numbers 6:24–26). Relying on God's strength and provision, you will be able to continue on, moving forward in hope.

As you do that, you may find yourself in uncharted waters, never having traveled this way before. But even so, you will find yourself getting stronger every day. As time passes, you will discover your grief will become less intense. That doesn't mean your affection for the one you love has diminished. Don't fear healing because you think it might lessen the impact your loved one has had on your life. Instead, realize that God continues to heal your hurt and to give you an abundant life here on earth. Your loved one wouldn't want you to miss out on that!

As you carry the one you love with you in your heart and mind, God will grow your faith and deepen your love for others. He will use you to bring comfort and hope to those who find themselves wandering through a season of grief. When that opportunity comes along, you can invite those who grieve to join you in leaning on Jesus in hope. You may even share with them the good news you received today:

The LORD is near to the brokenhearted and saves the crushed in spirit.

Psalm 34:18

The Lord himself is your strength!

Concluding Prayer

Dear Lord,
I want to remember your words,
words that tell me that you'll give me
enough strength simply to make it through this day
Some days I need a lot.
I know you realize that.
And I realize you will be my strength
when I have none of my own.
You will give me strength for each day.
The journey is too much for me.
Nothing is too much for you.
Lead me through this season of grief.
Lead me through the intensity of my pain.
Lead me through it all.
Please.
I can't see beyond the fog right now,
but I'll trust you.
You know what each tomorrow holds,
and you want what's best for me.
Lead on.
I'll follow, trusting. Amen.

Chapter Ten

Leaning on God's Word

"Your word is a lamp to my feet and a light to my path.

Psalm 119 : 105

Remember your word to your servant,
in which you have made me hope.
This is my comfort in my affliction,
that your promise gives me life.

Psalm 119 : 49—50

God speaks words of comfort in the Scriptures. Your Savior wants to make the "love notes" on the following pages personal and intimate. May they bless you, strengthen you, and bring you comfort.

The LORD bless you and keep you; the LORD make his face to shine upon you and be gracious to you; the LORD lift up his countenance upon you and give you peace.

Numbers 6:24–26

God is our refuge and strength, a very present help in trouble.

Psalm 46:1

For God alone my soul waits in silence;
from him comes my salvation.

Psalm 62 : 1

For I know the plans I have for you, declares
the LORD, plans for welfare and not for
evil, to give you a future and a hope.

Jeremiah 29 : 11

[Jesus said,] "I am with you always, to the
end of the age."

Matthew 28 : 20

[Jesus said,] "For God so loved the world, that he gave his only Son, that whoever believes in him should not perish but have eternal life."

John 3:16

[Jesus said,] "I am the resurrection and the life. Whoever believes in me, though he die, yet shall he live, and everyone who lives and believes in me shall never die."

John 11:25–26

"If God is for us, who can be against us? . . . For I am sure that neither death nor life, nor angels nor rulers, nor things present nor things to come, nor powers, nor height nor depth, nor anything else in all creation, will be able to separate us from the love of God in Christ Jesus our Lord.

Romans 8 : 31, 38—39

Be faithful unto death, and I will give you the crown of life.

Revelation 2 : 10

He will wipe away every tear from their eyes, and death shall be no more, neither shall there be mourning, nor crying, nor pain anymore, for the former things [will have] passed away. . . . I am making all things new.

Revelation 21:4–5

But we do not want you to be uninformed, brothers, about those who are asleep, that you may not grieve as others do who have no hope. For since we believe that Jesus died and rose again, even so, through Jesus, God will bring with him those who have fallen asleep.

1 Thessalonians 4:13–14

To see all of CTA's devotion books and journals, visit us at www.CTAinc.com. You may order online or by calling 1-800-999-1874. If this book has made a difference in your life or if you have simply enjoyed it, we would like to hear from you. Your words will encourage us!

Email: editor@CTAinc.com; include the subject
line: JCY22SC.

Write: Editorial Manager, Dept. JCY22SC
CTA, Inc.
PO Box 1205
Fenton, MO 63026-1205

Comment Online: ctainc.com (search JCY22SC)